DURGA

Once upon a time, there lived a demon king by the name of Rambha who fell in love with the princess Shyamala, who had been cursed to turn into a water buffalo.

Rambha and Shyamala had a son. King Rambha was filled with joy on seeing his son! He declared, 'My son shall prove to be the greatest king of the asuras. I shall name him Mahishasura!'

Mahishasura was part demon and part buffalo. He had mastered the art of stealth. He could change into any form that he desired. After being crowned the king of asuras, he wreaked havoc throughout the world!

Mahishasura desired immortality. However, it wasn't possible without the grace of the gods! He, thus, decided to invoke Lord Brahma and meditated for thousands of years.

At last, he was successful in pleasing Lord Brahma!

The Lord appeared before Mahishasura and said, 'I am pleased by your devotion. Ask what you desire and it shall be given.'

Mahishasura wasted no time. He asked Brahma for the boon of immortality. 'Let no man, animal or God kill me!' said Mahishasura.

Suddenly, Brahma's face lit up! Mahishasura was granted his boon. Armed with the boon of immortality, Mahishasura ravaged the earth and the heavens! This alarmed Lord Indra, the king of the devas. A long and fierce war occurred between the devas and the asuras. Mahishasura easily defeated Lord Indra.

Indra decided to take refuge with the supreme gods, the Trinity of Brahma, Vishnu and Shiva. The gods narrated their sorry situation. Indra pleaded to the Trinity, 'Please protect us from the tyrant, Mahishasura.'

The Trinity were annoyed at Mahishasura's audacity! An 'akashvani', a celestial voice, was heard.

'Lord Brahma's boon protects Mahishasura from being killed at the hands of a man or a god. Only a woman will be able to destroy him!'

Rays of light emanated from the bodies of Brahma, Vishnu, and Shiva, giving birth to the ten-armed warrior Goddess Durga, 'the invincible one'!

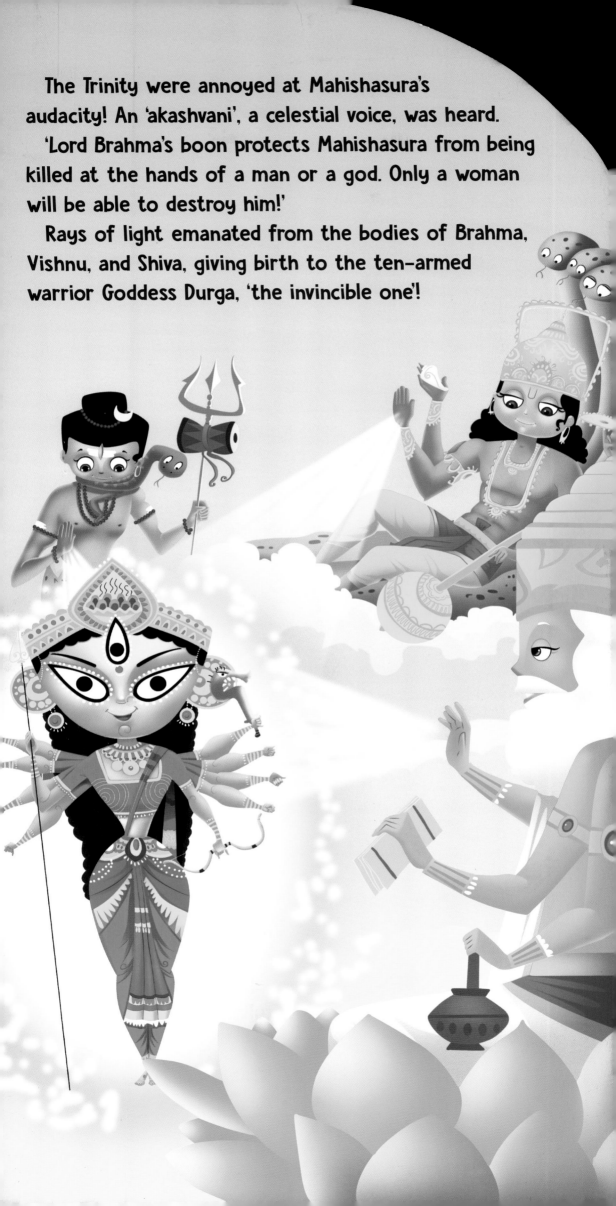

The gods gifted her a variety of weapons to fight Mahishasura. The celestial discus was given to her by Vishnu, the trident by Shiva and a pot of sacred water was given to her by Brahma. Lord Varuna gave her the conch shell. Kala gave her a sword. A bow and a quiver full of arrows were given to her by Vayu and Surya. A mace was given by Yama and a thunderbolt, by Indra. A spear by Agni and an axe by Vishwakarma, were gifted. The Himalayas gifted her with a lion to ride upon.

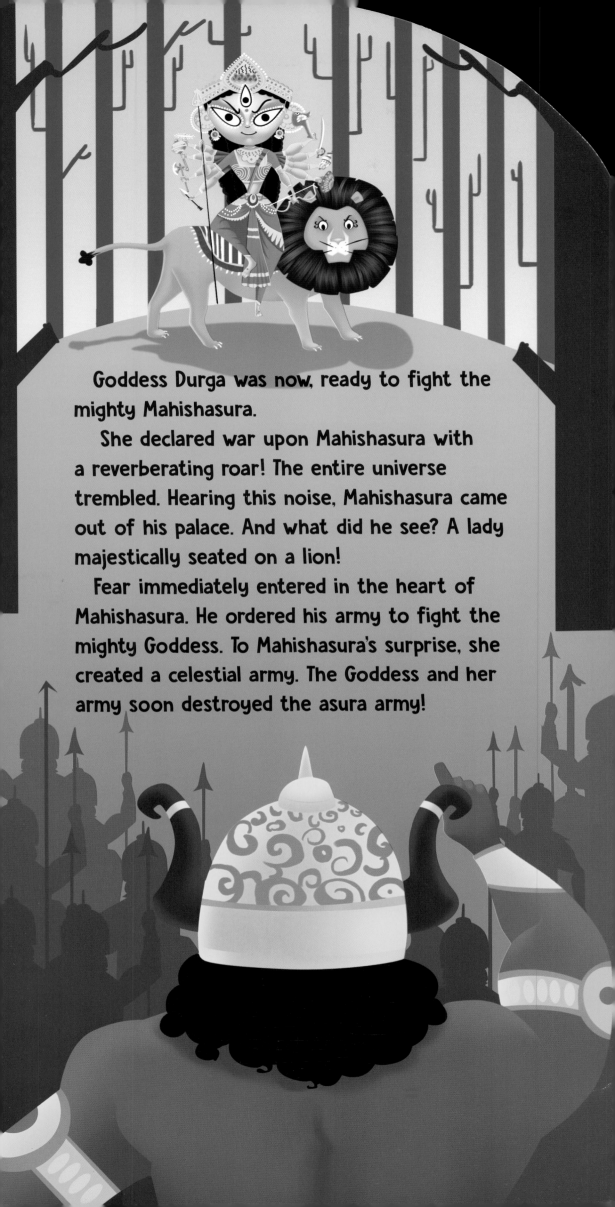

Goddess Durga was now, ready to fight the mighty Mahishasura.

She declared war upon Mahishasura with a reverberating roar! The entire universe trembled. Hearing this noise, Mahishasura came out of his palace. And what did he see? A lady majestically seated on a lion!

Fear immediately entered in the heart of Mahishasura. He ordered his army to fight the mighty Goddess. To Mahishasura's surprise, she created a celestial army. The Goddess and her army soon destroyed the asura army!

Mahishasura had no choice but to fight the Goddess on his own. A fierce battle ensued. He was a master of stealth and sometimes took the form of an elephant, a lion and finally, that of a buffalo to baffle the Goddess! The battle continued for nine days. On the tenth day, the Goddess slayed Mahishasura with her trident. The Goddess had done what no man or god could do. She had destroyed the root of evil.

The gods were overjoyed! They sang songs in praise of her. 'You are our protector,' they said. The Goddess blessed them and returned to her abode in the heavens.

She was now given the name of 'Mahishasuramardini', the slayer of Mahishasura and has been called upon when any being feels fear in their heart. She is celebrated as a kind-hearted mother and the universal protector of all goodness in the world.